Facsimiles

DANIEL HEALY

Published by Cinnamon Press
Meirion House
 Glan yr afon
Tanygrisiau
Blaenau Ffestiniog
Gwynedd
 LL41 3SU
www.cinnamonpress.com

The right of Daniel Healy to be identified as author of this work
has been asserted by him in accordance with the Copyright,
Designs and Patent Act, 1988. Copyright © 2010 Daniel Healy
ISBN: 978-1-907090-18-9
British Library Cataloguing in Publication Data. A CIP record for
this book can be obtained from the British Library.

Designed and typeset in Palatino by Cinnamon Press. Cover
design by Cottia Fortune-Wood from original artwork 'Tables' by
Jean Franc, agency © dreamstime.com

Printed in Poland.

Cinnamon Press is represented in the UK by Inpress Ltd
www.inpressbooks.co.uk and in Wales by the Welsh Books
Council www.cllc.org.uk.

The publisher acknowledges the financial support of the Welsh
Books Council.

Acknowledgements

Thanks to the editors of the journals in which some of these poems have appeared previously: *Anon, Borderlines, Bottlerockets, Chanticleer, Chimera, Dream Catcher, Envoi, Eildon Tree, Equinox, Fire, HQ, The Journal, Moodswing, Obsessed With Pipework, Orbis, Plainspoke, Poetry Cornwall, Poetry on the Lake, Quantum Leap, The Rialto, Seam, Seventh Quarry.*

Daniel Healy was born in 1972 in Wales. He's worked as a tote operator, machine operator, animal feed salesman, newspaper vendor, apple picker and big issue seller. He now works as a bookseller in Cambridge.

Contents

Facsimiles

to Ferdia

Origins

Watching
the moorland;

soft
waves of grass

hard
against the crag.

Waiting
for the shout,

the release
of echoes

hidden
in the stone.

Elsewhere

Thought slows
on the island

a place
without language,

unable to describe
the change of light,

of heat, thick
in the marrow,

the way
the dark cloud

folds the horizon
into waves,

the twist
of olive trees

fruit thin
around the stone,

the sparse
population of words.

Testimony

Borrowed air
stale on the tongue

the unspoken

words that burn
in the throat

the fragmented
bare remains.

A Landscape

The view
becomes scenic

the hint
of brush strokes

to the air
without cloud

pale and empty
the sun, flat

against the side
of the hill,

a backdrop,
the stillness of light,

in the foreground
a single tree,

liquid and green
with shadow,

its branches
vein the sky.

Vista

For once
the sky is perfect,

a collage
of half-remembered

images turning
the right

shade of blue.

Impression

Light rain
at the harbour

a cold wind
catches the nets

a woman's hair
black with water

the cut of waves
mapping the air.

Foundations

The hail,
the change of light

picks out the ruins,
re-shapes the landscape

in brief fragments
raised from the earth,

the field,
a sea of frozen waves

beneath your feet
the tenderness of glass.

Waking

To a bare room
in winter

to the window,
reflected sunlight
hard with shadow

cuts the glass,
the bright frost,
brings a taste

to the air,
to the tongue
that pulls

like the stick
of cold metal.

Littoral

Last night
I dreamt of you,

of waking
to your touch.

This morning
I wake

to the sound
of autumn rain

make its patterns
in the leaves.

Drowning

Trees
dense with light

the heat,
the stillness

at the centre
measuring the air

the thick
pattern of leaves

a tenuous
thread of sky.

The Moorland

The boulder
wind-scoured
cracks in stone

between rocks
the hard
gristle of land

the thin
ribboned earth
cut by water

the flense
of rain
paring the bone.

Transient

At sunset
passing through
a mountain town's
drizzle of streets

on mellowed stone
like seamed skin
the softened, slow
glide of rain.

After the Rain

The sound
and scent of woods
crowding the alley

the rough
grain of brick
dark and smoothed

by water
drips from thin metal
branched against the sky.

Exterior

The serrated
edge of roofs
cut the morning,

a sharp-winged
bleed of shadows;
dark birds rising.

The View

A tactile gaze
pauses

on the pitted
railings

along the sea-
front.

Fruit

You are eating
a pomegranate

and talking
about something

apt, I'm sure.
I'm not listening

simply nodding
to the rhythm

and bite
of your words,

watching the slow
clot of seeds

as they form
between your teeth.

At Noon

The stunted
twist of trees

the roughened
scar of a table

the fruit, quartered,
pale flesh opened

across the dark
stain of wood.

Coastal

In late afternoon,
white above the green,

the washing
hanging in spring rain,

within clean sheets
a thin breeze traces

the cool hollow
of your throat,

an imposed landscape,
the hills, the soft

glide of muscle
to the sea

the scent of your skin,
a ripple of light

on the distant, variegated,
dark heart of waves.

Beached

In a drizzled
reflection of light
a ruined boat

pulled high,
swollen with memory
and split wood,

I peel away
the splinters, soft
under hard nails,

a calloused touch
meeting the still
pliant heart,

the slow pull
of last resistance.

Canal

On the once black
smooth water

the pockmarked
open sores of rain.

The Visit

Waking
in late morning

to the remains
of a still life

hot cups of coffee
grown cold

eyes caught
on the bright peel

of oranges
scattered on the frost

resisting the urge
to reclaim

I sit,
I peel the fruit

and I drink
my coffee hot.

Disinterest

The rain falls
in its accustomed
patterns

makes slick reflections
on black slate,
on dark water,

slides the light,
blurs the window
at which

you brush your hair,
each movement assured
accustomed to habit.

Pausing

In the clearing
only the tips move;

sparse leaves, slight grass
tracing the air,

the scent of moss,
a thin breeze articulates.

Now

& then
with the unreliable
perfection of memory

I allow myself
a form of nostalgia

a feeling
akin to vertigo

remembering
the curve of your breast
the line of a neck
your scent

& no matter
how rare the glimpse

it seems
that I'm sketching

the shape of a ghost
between us.

Replacing

Your worn tools
in the box

my eyes tracing
the smooth grain
of the wood

I remember
the whorl
of your thumb

the way veins
climbed your hands

the thick scars
the black nails

and other
clichéd poems
about fathers.

Reading

Your name in the graveyard
past the rust of lichen

slow, dark spots of rain
create their shadows on the stone.

The Cottage

This morning
attempting

the inexact
description of place,

this moment,
the rain falls

on slick grass,
the earth still dry.

Your coffee cup
white on the sill.

The watermarked
change of light

shadows your face,
a dark room claims you.

Thirst

In late summer
at the lake

waiting to hear
the smooth sound

of waves
after sunset

a soft breeze
carries

only the rattle
of dry reeds.

Hotel Room

A hard frost
through glass
cold & brittle

to the eye
in the rooms
warm darkness

the ghost
of pale limbs
turning

a smoothed
& distant
perfection

in the morning's
bright failure
of words.

From Memory

The dark
slate of roofs

staple
the valley,

the road
scars its line.

Waiting
for the tear,

the sound
as a wound opens.

Repeating Mistakes

Flicking through
the memories
that have made me

I find the colours
faded, surfaces
cracked from over use,

with an unwelcome
sense of drifting
I pick up the pen
and begin to re-touch.

The Tide

slips in
on thin waves

quick & deliberate,
sharp

against the beach:
a sickle of light

before the encrusted
scabs of rock.

Outline

The ruin,
the bare suggestion
of shape

dictates content.
A stone sill
makes solid

the glass,
the dark interior.
The sun,

a weak gesture
of light
attempts reflection.

A breeze
cuts the silence,
brings the scent

of heather
slight rain
and cold earth.

The sky,
a gathered promise
edges the horizon.

The Gaze

Follows
the landscape,

the expected
slow fall
of the hill

to the edge,
to the solid
roots of houses

through trees
heavy with green
the bright

flicker of deer
unsettles the eye.

The Return

From above, the land,
grasping

the shape
of a twisted fist.

Deep-knuckled points.
The disjointed,

crushed,
hollows of bone.

A secret,
hidden, in the palm.

Becalmed

In the first
grey wash of light

through the window
the sight of you,

the beach, the harbour's
narrowed throat,

the slight swell
of ingrown waves

constrained, the hard-packed
tight grains of sand

that have refused
to accept your steps.

Above the River

Mist,
the bridge,

soft
ribs of metal;

the illusion
of breath

damp
and cold

against
your face,

the coughed
bloody

flecks
of rust.

Reclining

In late
afternoon

you become
a sculpture

placed
in the turn

of light
from the window

the stillness
of your limbs

your skin
the muscled

sleep of stone
aching to touch.

Twilight

In the orchard

dark lines
against the grey

the scent of a branch
fresh-cut

sweeter
than the fruit.

Leaving Town

From the train
passing the outskirts
crooked and unplanned

pathways narrowed
by black nettles

the evening and metal
gilded with rust

the deepening sky
and thinning cloud
reflections shattered in glass.

Near Evening

Revisiting
the shore line

expecting change
in the damp

whisper of grass
heavy with salt.

Glass, scattered
on the beach

retains a dull
memory of shape

made smooth
and safe to hold.

& Again

Returning
to the coast

to the grey sea,
a window

& October's
unleavened cloud.

In the Evening

The lake, man-made,
its shallow ripples
contained, repeating,
the water obeys.

A lowered sky
in dark reflection,
the crouching
shadow of hills.

Turning away
I reduce the landscape,
twisting it to fit
my own expectation.

Amber

Late evening,
the day slows
to a resin of light.

Beyond the window
in slight rain
the cars moored
to the pavement
settle above reflection

releasing the dim sight
of figures, of people
moving, their dark
shapes reduced
to bubbles in the glass.

Late Evening

In the meadow
bright colours fade
into scent,

seed heads blur
in a light breeze;

flowers of smoke
above the grass.

After the Frost

a cold wind

grey waves
& sand dunes

on the railing
salt & blistered paint

leeched of colour

the immaculate
clear sky.

Unearthed

Amongst the roots
gripping the rock

sharp, flakes of stone
cutting deep.

In Recollection

Shallow earth
stains the rock,

wind grazes the land,
splits the grasses,

a single tree
stands twisted

an image
made, dependent.

The soft cloud,
the sunlight,

the flowers
I did not mention.

Aftermath

A sky
of brushed steel.

A wind-
scoured day

of anaemic cloud
& pale grass.

The rivers
dulled blade.

The buildings,
shapeless,

a blur
of faded stone.

Passing
associations lost.

Through cold air
& empty reeds

the floating husk
of wheat fields.

Stillness after the storm
the once tidal fields
of corn grown silent

Unseeing

In the bare
winter garden
waiting for snow
to give shape
to the dull
smoke of evening,

there is only
the slur of rain
over empty paths
and raked gravel:
a consequence
of mannered perception.

Watching

The rocks
at sunset;

the exposed
muscle of land,

those torn
hump-backed

islands rising
from the grass

flex and shift
in the passing

of light, unsteadies
the step, removes

the expectation
of firm ground.

Midwinter

Crossing the bridge
above

the half-seen
movement

of cold, dark
shapes

the slow
ripple of focus

the river
marbled with ice.

Sketching

Only your gaze moves
across a cold landscape

deep with snow,
your stick

of charcoal poised
above a blank sheet.

From a copse of winter trees
the spiralled tracery of crows.

Transition

Night closes
like a fist
around the
ruined farmhouse
in the valley,

long shadows
curl over
half-formed brick
past veins
of ivy,

a suggestion
of shape,
broken knuckles
blurred
against the sky.

I had thought to write

I had thought
to write

about the rain
beading down,

the similarities
of water & glass,

the separation
of an open window.

Instead
I had to mention

the thickening
of winter,

the sleet
& the pearls of hail.